MICROSOFT

For Beginners 2022

The A-Z Guide for beginners and seniors.

Howard J. Wall

i

Introduction to Microsoft Teams

Microsoft Teams is the greatest business chat app available. It's a place for real-time communication and collaboration, as well as meetings, file and app sharing, and even a few emoticons. Everyone can see them since they are all in one area and out in the open. Whatever you're working on, you can use Microsoft Teams to get things done with your team or with friends and family. It is said to be the only program that combines all of these features in one spot. Make plans come to life by connecting with people fast through group chat.

This is how you can go about doing it. Get your family and friends together to help with chores at home or plan a birthday surprise. With built-in cloud storage, you can work with your coworkers in private meetings, make video calls, and share documents with them. In

Microsoft Teams, you can do everything you want to do.

It's easy to connect with anyone:

- You can use video calling to meet with your teammates, family, and friends in a safe way. People can join a video meeting by sharing a link or a calendar invite. With friends or coworkers, you can talk to each other one on one, or you can have group chats.
- Dedicated group messaging channels help keep important projects in the same place at the same time.
- You can video call anyone in Teams, or you can make a group chat video call right away. Make it easier to say what you mean when words can't do it. GIFs, emojis, message animations, and other types of animations can help.

- Whether you're looking for a work chat or groups chat for your friends and family, Microsoft Teams makes communication easy and convenient for everyone, no matter what.

As a group, make plans and do projects.

- Task lists help you keep track of work projects or plans with family and friends. To keep everyone on the same page, assign tasks, set due dates, and cross off tasks that have been done.

- Working together on work or personal projects is easier with file sharing in conversations. Furthermore, cloud storage makes it simple to access shared documents and files when on the go. So you don't have to waste time looking for things, the Dashboard view elegantly organizes all shared stuff, such as images, files, projects, and links. To get the most out of your meetings, screen sharing, draw on a whiteboard, or break up into virtual rooms is a fantastic idea.

For your own peace of mind, consider the following:

1. Collaborate on work tasks with outside partners while maintaining control over your data. This means that you should keep important information like subscription passwords in a digital Safe*, like this one.

2. The kind of security and compliance you expect from Microsoft 365 When you use Microsoft Teams with your own account.
   If you want to use the commercial features of this app, you'll need to pay for it or try Microsoft Teams for work. If you don't know if your company has a subscription to Office or what services you can use, go to

Office.com/Teams to find out or talk to your IT team.

CHAPTER 1

GETTING STARTED WITH MICROSOFT TEAMS

Teams is a central center for workplace conversations, collaborative teamwork, video conferencing, and document sharing, all of which are aimed to improve worker productivity in a unified set of Microsoft 365 and Office 365 technologies. Slack rival Microsoft saw its use of Teams soar to 75 million active users a day in April as the COVID-19 outbreak progressed, according to Microsoft numbers disclosed at the time. Using the term "fastest-growing business app," the corporation referred to Teams.

It is no surprise that, since its inception, Microsoft Teams has become a more prominent aspect of the company's office productivity and collaboration strategy. As Raul Castanon, senior analyst at 451 Research Global Market Intelligence, noted, "Teams has emerged as a star product rather than an add-on" Using Teams to link employees and their apps, especially those who work remotely, might serve as an alternative or even a replacement for email communication. As a Microsoft official put it, think of it as a "digital translation of an open office area. Dux Raymond Sy, chief brand officer, Microsoft MVP, and regional director of Microsoft partner AvePoint, described the collaborative workplace as a "essential hole" filler for Microsoft 365 apps. For Microsoft, an integrated hub integrating persistent chat, files, and videoconferencing together was the future of workplace collaboration from the outset, says Sy. A desktop client, a web browser add-on, and a mobile app are all options for using Teams. It's compatible with all major operating systems, including Windows, Mac OS X, iOS, and the Android platform.

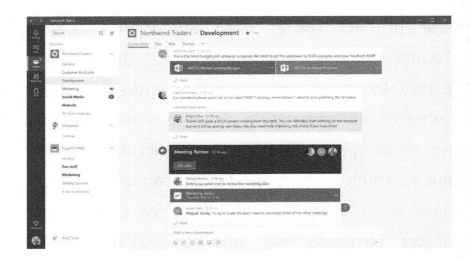

Each team has a set of "channels" that focus on a specific thing, like a work project or a certain subject. Channels are group chat rooms that are better for fast-paced conversations than e-mails. Private and "regular" channels are the two basic types of channels. Private channels are useful for private communications, which are beneficial to legal and finance teams. Everyone in a workspace can see what has been written and access shared files using "standard" channels.

There is currently a "general" channel, but admins can build others to match the needs of their team. You don't have to switch screens to work because each channel contains tabs with shared files and apps. According to a Forrester analysis, teams can dramatically reduce app switching, saving each employee 15 to 25 minutes each day. In addition to using group chats in a channel, workers can send private messages to their coworkers, or they can start a new group conversation and invite other people to join in on the fun. Teams has all the features you'd expect from a business chat app, like emojis, GIFs, rich text editing, @mentions, threaded conversations, bots, and the ability to share files. At the touch of a button, users can switch from texting to making a video call. When a conversation is important, it can be put at the top of the chat list.

Users who have previously used a collaborative tool should be able to navigate with ease, while those who are making the switch from email for the first time may require some time to adjust to the UI. The navigation arrows, search bar, and app launcher are all located in the top bar. This allows users to quickly access messages, files, and other members of their organization. It's possible to change your availability status from the menu on the right-hand side.

The desktop app has a sidebar to the left that contains shortcuts to the most frequently used features of Teams. All of these apps are grouped together in a single Activity news feed, which displays mentions and answers. Apps that have been approved by Microsoft and third-party developers can also be found in the Teams app store. To further personalize the left-hand bar, you can use third-party and Microsoft 365 apps.

Microsoft Teams: How to use it for work

Users of Teams can collaborate on papers as well as communicate in real time. When it comes to productivity apps, Microsoft has an advantage over its competitors since it serves as a hub or connector to the rest of Microsoft 365's capabilities.

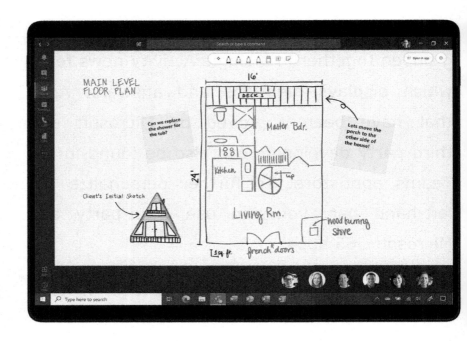

With Microsoft Office tools and Microsoft Whiteboard, teams can work together in real time without switching screens. Co-editing Word, Excel, PowerPoint, and other file types in real-time is possible without having to leave Teams. OneDrive is used to store and access files in the "files" part of the app. (Box and Egnyte are other alternatives.) In order to give easy access to calendars and schedule meetings, Teams integrates with Outlook calendars. Yammer, the business social networking program, is fully integrated with Teams via the Communities app, and SharePoint material can be accessed from within Teams. Microsoft has also announced new Teams-specific applications this year. To replace Planner in Teams, "Tasks" was introduced earlier this year. It combines features from the Planner and To Do apps. A number of views, including Kanban-style cards, can be used to track individual and team-based work in Tasks (which is still called Planner for now).

Additionally, Lists is a database and spreadsheet tool that may be used to plan events, track recruitment, or help new staff get up and running. Office workers aren't the only ones who can use Teams. Microsoft has been increasing its focus on "first-line workers," such as field technicians, retail personnel, and hospital workers, in recent years.

How to use Microsoft Teams: Video and voice meetings

A team has virtually replaced Microsoft's widely used Skype for Business Online program with video and audio conferencing. In the wake of the pandemic, companies scrambled to set up virtual meetings with faraway employees. This month Microsoft claimed a 1000 percent rise in the number of daily active Teams users, going from 32 million at the beginning of March to 75 million at the end of April. Working from home is now possible thanks to Microsoft Teams, as Sy pointed out. Videoconferencing, screen-sharing, and the ability to effortlessly collaborate and co-work on files are all enabling firms and their employees to be even more productive than they were pre-pandemic."

New features have been implemented swiftly by Microsoft in order to take advantage of the rapid shift in work habits and alleviate videoconference fatigue. There have been a number of big changes in the app since the beginning of the year, including the launch of the "Together" mode this summer, which allows users to gather together in a virtual meeting room or café and share their video feeds. In September, Microsoft rolled out even more sceneries and layouts like this. More natural-feeling video meetings can be achieved through the use of simulated "scenes" provided by Microsoft Together mode. We've included in real-time noise suppression to assist keep you focused. Deep-learning techniques are used to remove all except the spoken signal from the surrounding noise.

Basic video conference features, such as custom backdrops, screen sharing, raising hands, recording and live captions, are available to teams. Additionally, Teams may be used for company-wide broadcasts, which can include up to 10,000 employees with a live video feed (or 20,000 with the Advanced Communications license add-on). Cloud voicemail, call queues, direct routing to existing telecoms providers, and audio conferencing are all included in audio call functionality.

Microsoft Teams: Integrations and automations

As expected, Microsoft falls short of Slack in terms of the sheer number of third-party app connectors it offers. Even so, Microsoft's app directory was launched in 2018 and features a wide selection of third-party integrations. Many types of apps are available in the app store, including personal ones such as chatbots and messaging apps. It is possible to use these in a variety of ways. A connector posts data from an external service into a channel using "tab" apps, for example. Mind mapping and creative planning tools like Mindmeister and Mural are among the most popular apps, as are IT and developer-focused solutions such as ServiceDesk; Bitbucket and PagerDuty; and Trello. Using Teams' developer platform, developers may also design and integrate their own internal apps, bots, and tabs. During a video call, Microsoft is also allowing third-party app developers to integrate their own applications into the Teams meeting experience.

Teams offers no-code and low-code alternatives for creating apps and customized workflows. Project Oakdale allows users to "develop, deploy, distribute, utilize, and administrate Power Apps solutions" without leaving Teams while custom business apps created with Microsoft's low-code Power Apps tool may be integrated into Teams. And Power Virtual Agents allows users to create chatbots without writing any code. Users can establish "flows" in Power Automate to automate operations, such as approving a document, from within the Teams platform.

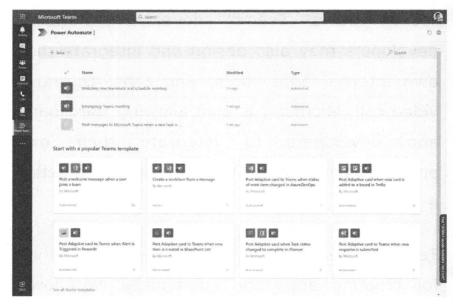

How to disable Microsoft Teams auto-launch

Instead of erasing Teams completely, you may wish to turn them off. Despite the fact that many businesses rely on Office 365 technologies, many employees do not want the Teams app to be launched automatically when their computers are turned on for some reason.

Launch the Teams app, click the initials icon in the upper-right corner, and select settings to make the adjustment. Uncheck "Auto-start application" in the General settings area, as well as "Open in background" and "On close, keep application running." It is also feasible for Windows 10 users to disable auto-launch from the Start menu. When you log in to a device, you'll get a list of all the apps that are automatically launched. Locate the Teams app and simply tap the "off" button.

Additionally, users who just want to avoid the application's messages can minimize the amount of alerts they receive. Select Notifications in the settings menu. You can turn off notification noises and select which events, such as chat answers, mentions and reactions, or meeting reminders, will trigger notifications from this menu. Several Windows 10 customers have reported that Teams has resurfaced despite their belief that it had been permanently eliminated from the operating system. This appears to be the result of consumers failing to completely remove the application from their devices. The Teams app and the Teams Machine-Wide Installer are the two pieces of software that must be deleted in order to completely uninstall Teams. Upon rebooting Windows, it's the second piece of software that will immediately restore Team's services.

11 best practices for Microsoft Teams video meetings

Your coworkers may use Microsoft Teams for text chats, but as more and more office workers across the world are working from their homes, video meetings are becoming increasingly important. Despite the fact that older clients can still use Skype for Business, Microsoft has integrated its features into Teams, which are now part of Microsoft 365/Office365 subscriptions for businesses and enterprises. Whether it's an informal video chat with your coworkers or a client presentation, there are methods to improve the experience for you and the other participants. Before, during, and after your video meeting, here are some recommended practices for using Teams to its fullest potential. Using the Calendar icon in the left toolbar, you can begin setting up a video conference with your Team members. Calendars appear in your Teams workspace's main pane. The New meeting button is located at the top right of the screen. When you click "New meeting," the "New meeting" screen will appear on top of the main window. If your company's address book is integrated with Teams, you can simply start typing the names of the attendees and select from the list that appears after you've given the meeting a title. The Optional option at the right of the attendee's field lets you invite individuals without making it mandatory that they show up. Simply type their names in the "Optional" form that displays.

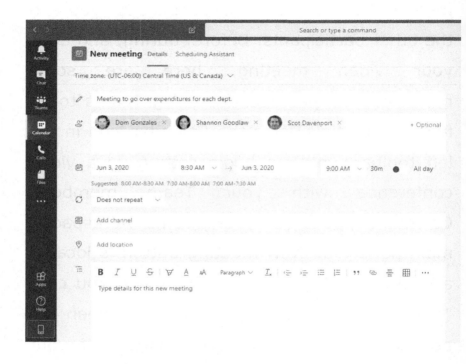

To begin, select a date, a time, and a finish time on the following line. However, there are a few more steps you can take to make your invitation stand out, which we'll go over next. To send the invitation, click Save in the upper right corner when you're through setting up the meeting.

1. Adjust the time of your meeting

It's a good idea to simply schedule a meeting and see if any of the other participants object. There is a better way: Click the Scheduling Assistant tab at the top of the "New meeting" page. The mandatory and optional attendees you've invited will be listed on the page's left side, along with their availability status: Available, Unavailable, or Unknown. In order to get this data, you need to know what your guests have scheduled in their Outlook calendar. There is a calendar view on your right that shows all of your scheduled meetings in purple.

Once you select a date and time for your meeting, Teams will automatically look for alternate dates and times if they are available.

Start and end timings are located at the top of your screen, while suggested meeting times can be found right below. Replace the start and finish dates that you initially entered by clicking on one of these suggested start and end times. To determine if another day is less congested than the one you originally selected, you can scroll through the days in the schedule view. Click the date and the start/end times at the top of the page to change them if you find a time that works for everyone.

2. Make a copy of the agenda for your meeting.

When organizing a meeting, it's a good idea to include the meeting agenda so that everyone knows what to expect and how to prepare. A message box is located at the bottom of the "New meeting" screen, where you can type in a message to be included in the meeting invitation. In order to keep the meeting information in the invitation email from being overshadowed by a lengthy agenda, we recommend that you keep it to a manageable length here (e.g., a table or a bulleted list).

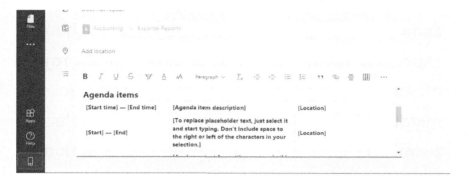

A concise meeting agenda aids attendees in getting ready for the gathering. (Click on the image to enlarge it.)) Send a separate email with a.doc or PDF file attached, or submit a reply to the meeting announcement message in a channel with the agenda attached as specified below if you're hosting the meeting in a channel.

3. Use a channel to hold your meeting.

There are times when a "open" meeting hosted in a certain channel in Teams is more appropriate than a meeting with specific people you've invited. The meeting will be open to all members of the channel. This functionality may come in handy if you have set up a channel especially for the purpose of conducting project meetings. Using the drop-down menu in the middle of the "New meeting" screen, select a team and a channel from the available options.

The ability to host a meeting in a channel means that anyone who is a subscriber to that channel can attend the meeting. (Click on the image to enlarge it.)) A message is posted to the channel's Posts tab and an email invitation is sent to each member of the channel after you finish organizing your meeting and click Send. Responses may include files and other pertinent information from any participant of the channel. The details of the meeting can be found on the Posts tab of the channel. You can attach a meeting agenda as a document to your own meeting notification by replying to it (such as a .doc or PDF file). Your invitees and channel members will appreciate you if you provide them with this information ahead of time.

4. Perform a hardware test.

Create a test call before your first Teams video meeting so that you may test your device's compatibility with the platform. Allowing Teams access to your computer's microphone, speakers, and camera may need you to provide rights in many places, such as in System Preferences on current Mac OS X versions. Do you intend to show the meeting participants your screen? This may also necessitate a different authorization. Now is the time to put everything in place and put it to the test.

It's also a good idea to remind anyone joining via video call for the first time to come ten minutes early. You can begin the meeting early so that everyone has time to set up their equipment before the designated start time. We had a meeting and Use a backdrop image or blur the background. Professional image is essential in video meetings, and that includes what is seen behind you. Simply said, Microsoft's background blur feature accomplishes exactly what it claims to do. Alternatively, you can choose from a gallery of pre-installed background photos provided by Microsoft. Making your image stand out from the rest of the room is easier with the use of a blurred background or an image as a background.

Before you attend a planned meeting, use the following steps to enable backdrop blur or a background image: Second switch down on video preview, where you may see yourself on camera (the headshot icon). On the right, a "Background settings" pane displays. You can enable background blur by selecting one of the blurred photos in the upper right corner of the screen, or by selecting a different background image to show in front of the blurred one. However, Microsoft has stated that it will be possible for users to upload their own personalized background image in the future.

In order to activate a backdrop effect while already in a meeting, follow these steps: The meeting controls toolbar will appear above your video stream when you move the cursor over it. Open the "More actions" menu by clicking the three-dot icon, then select "Show background effects". "Background settings" pane will appear as seen above. To see what you'll look like in the meeting before you turn on video, click Preview first. Then click Apply to turn on video and see how it appears to the rest of the group.

Be aware that Teams' backdrop effects may not work with some models of front-facing cameras in laptops and other devices, including webcams. There are a few things to keep in mind while using backdrop effects.

5. Share your screen, but not too much.

You don't have to share your entire desktop if you only need to share a certain application running on your PC (such as an Excel spreadsheet). As a result of this, your attendees will focus on only what you want them to see. You'll also be able to keep your personal information private, since they won't be able to view any open calendar or e-mail apps on your desktop. To share a running application window on your PC, click the Share icon in the meeting controls toolbar (the arrow over a rectangle). There will be a panel at the bottom of the screen. Program windows are displayed as thumbnails in the "Window" category. When you're in a meeting, you can share an app window by clicking on the app window.

The Share pane's other options are also worth noting. Additionally, you can open an interactive whiteboard for your meeting participants to mark up; share a PowerPoint presentation; or browse Teams, OneDrive, or your computer to share a file.

6. Using live captions is a good idea.

Teams' built-in closed captioning tool can aid those in your meeting who are hard of hearing, don't speak English fluently, or for any other reason have difficulty hearing the audio. Real-time captions display below the video feed as a result of voice recognition technology.

The Teams desktop and mobile apps let users to toggle on live captioning for them, but the web interface does not. A three-dot icon in the meeting controls toolbar will bring up the "More actions" option, where you can choose to turn on live subtitles. For now, live captions are only available if you're speaking English; they're currently being tested. However, a group of editors from Computerworld recently tested the feature and found it to be extremely accurate.

7. Make a copy of your meeting minutes.

Meetings are prone to omissions, but they can be simply recorded. You and your coworkers will have access to the video file via Microsoft's Stream cloud service. Anyone who was unable to attend the meeting can benefit from this, as well as anyone who wants a refresher on what was covered. Move your pointer to the meeting controls toolbar, click on the three-dot icon to open the "More actions" option, and select Start recording from it to record your meeting. The others at the meeting will notice a banner alerting them to the fact that the meeting is being taped.

By clicking the three-dot icon and selecting Stop recording, you can stop recording at any moment. It may take a while for the recording to be processed and saved to the Stream, but once it is, you and anyone else invited to the meeting will be able to view it. In the following section, we'll discuss that.)

8. Taking notes from the meeting.

Important points and action items are frequently forgotten after a meeting has ended, and it's not unusual for this to happen. Taking notes during the meeting and saving them as part of the meeting in Teams can help you maintain track of these items. Because they're saved with the meeting, it's simple to go back and look at them.

9. Move the cursor to summon the meeting controls toolbar, click the three-dot icon to open the "More actions" option, and pick Show meeting notes. Teams have a "Meeting notes" pane on the right side of the window. Take notes by clicking the Take notes icon. Make your text stand out by using the various formatting options available in the toolbar that appears when you do so. You can add a section headline by clicking the plus sign. You can make as many sections as you need to keep your notes organized in your notes app or notebook. If you click on the three-dot icon next to any part of the list, you can move it up or down in the list.

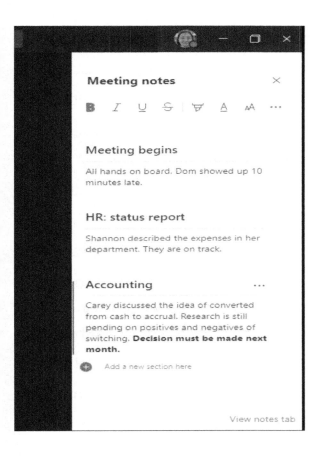

10. Allows you to make the recording available to others. Team members can see the video of a meeting that you've recorded, and you can see it as well. Aren't you supposed to remind your team that they can watch the footage at any time? There is a Chat button in the left toolbar that you can click on to access it. Anyone who is in the vicinity can access it simply by clicking on it. Select the meeting in which you captured the video from the drop-down menu adjacent to the toolbar. Click on the video to watch it. A thumbnail image of the video will appear in the meeting's Chat window. The video begins when you click on the thumbnail.

Additionally, you can access your scheduled meeting by selecting Calendar from the left toolbar, then going to the Chat tab at the very top of the window. A screenshot of a recording appears on the page as soon as you open the tab.everyone who attended the meeting can view the video via Microsoft Stream, and if the meeting was hosted in a channel, the video can be found under the Posts tab. Anyone who wasn't present at the meeting can't see or hear what was said during the meeting because the recording was only made by the individual who made it. Here are a few ideas: Click the three-dot icon next to the thumbnail on your Chat tab page, and then pick Share from the menu that displays, to share the video with everyone in your organization. To send the video to everyone in your organization, simply click the "Share" button. The three-dot icon next to the thumbnail of the video lets you receive the link to the video. Click the Copy button to copy the text. This link can be included in an email and sent to specific individuals.

You may also select "Open in Microsoft Stream" from the drop-down menu by clicking the three-dot icon next to the thumbnail of the movie. Meeting recordings will be available in Stream. Sharing links, emailing a group of people or getting embed code are all options you have when you click the Share button. Make a copy of the meeting minutes and distribute it to everyone. The meeting notes you've taken are also available in Teams. Click Chat in the left toolbar. To view the notes from your meeting, first choose it and then click the Meeting Notes tab. To see the meeting notes in full screen, click Calendar in the left toolbar, select your meeting, click the Chat tab, look for the announcement of the meeting notes, and then click Show notes in full screen. Additionally, if you held the meeting in a channel, the meeting notes will appear in the Posts tab as a reply to the original post announcing the meeting.

Adding notes from a different application, such as Microsoft Word, to a meeting or a message in the channel is feasible.

Your team will benefit from a meeting tape and the meeting notes, which will assist them, remember what was discussed and ensure that action items aren't overlooked. Make certain that your team has the ability to look at both.

CHAPTER 2

HOW TO NAVIGATE MICROSOFT TEAMS

In today's world, remote collaboration is more critical than ever before. These days, companies hunt for and find solutions to enable their employees to remain connected from everywhere they work. With Microsoft Teams, you'll be able to send and receive video messages, arrange video conference meetings, send and receive instant messages, exchange files, and more all from a single platform. We've witnessed a rise in interest in Microsoft Teams both internally and with our clients, which is why ***I wanted to show you around the Microsoft Teams UI.*** There's no better way to get a sense of how Teams looks and functions than by watching the video and reading the accompanying article below, which provides a fast tour of the product's tabs and features.

Main Screen

When you first open the application, you'll most likely see this page. When you access the Chat tab, the most recent chat conversation will be shown in the center of the screen. If you've linked or integrated other programs into Teams, you'll see tabs for those applications on the left-hand side of the page. Additionally, you'll find links to the App Store and Help in the menu that follows. It's possible to personalize your Teams interface by clicking the three horizontal dots and selecting new applications from a menu that appears.

The name and current status of the person currently logged in (in this case, it's me) may be seen in the upper right corner of the screen (online, offline, etc.). If you look immediately below it, you'll either find a "Join" button to start a video conference right away or three buttons to start a video call, audio call, or screen sharing depending on your preferences and the type of chat you've selected. To make an audio call, simply tap the "Start Audio Call" button in the chat you're currently participating in. You'll notice a search box at the top of the page, which we'll go into more detail about later.

Search Bar

At the very top of the page, in what amounts to an Omni-search bar of sorts, you can look for just about everything that Microsoft Teams has access to. As soon as you start entering a few letters, you'll see how this works. Three of my contacts and an application were retrieved using just two letters in the video. Using the Teams search bar, you can easily find individuals, apps, files, or anything else you're looking for.

Activity

The Activity tab is easy to understand. It shows you any notifications that might be important to you, like mentions, replies, and more.

Chat

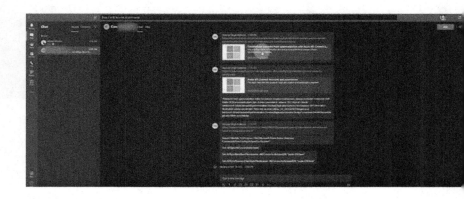

Chat is the primary window via which you can converse with other players. The video shows that I'm in conversation with a few different people and groups.

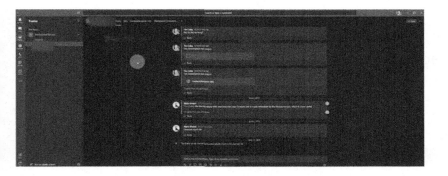

A team chat is the main window that shows a lot of how Teams works. I have a OneNote window open when I click on that group in the video. As a team, we can talk in a general chat, and any files that have been shared show up there. In addition to that, if you've used SharePoint before, there is also a way to store and share files.

You can even talk to people outside of your company. There is a Microsoft representative in the video that isn't part of Kelser, but we had been working with a Microsoft product. As long as other people use Microsoft Teams, you can work together with them. It's a powerful feature, but you might not want to use it right away. To make sure that it doesn't happen again, you can put a lock on the back end.

Video and Voice Calling

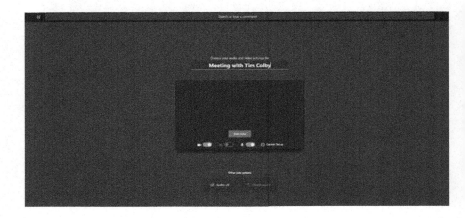

All of these functionalities are available on the Teams platform. While some of these choices were mentioned earlier (clicking on a contact and selecting "Join," or using the "Start video conference," "phone call," or screen share buttons), you can also add other contacts to those spur of the moment gatherings or even book them for later. You can also utilize the Teams VoIP capability to make phone calls. Additionally, Microsoft offers SIP trucking and a real telephone line for an extra monthly charge. Because it's still in its infancy, I can't suggest it to anyone who already uses a VoIP platform. In contrast, for someone like myself, who works from home in a basement with intermittent mobile reception, having an internal phone system has been a godsend. The knowledge that I can always communicate with my coworkers "over the phone" is a comforting one.

Calendar

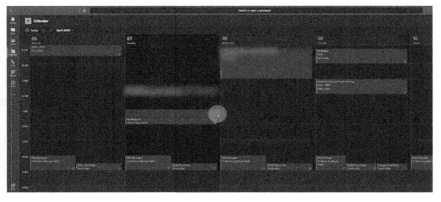

The Calendar tab, like the Chat tab, does pretty much what you'd expect. It opens up a calendar view. All of my calendar information is synchronized across all of the programs I use. This is because I have my Microsoft 365 account linked to it. It's another simple feature that shows how important collaboration and unification are to the Teams app. By syncing with my Microsoft 365 account, I don't have to check multiple apps for the same information and that information also feeds into other functions of the app (for example, if I wanted to have an impromptu meeting with someone, I could see their availability in Teams instead of having to check a different app entirely).

Apps and Other Applications

If you've added any more apps to your interface, you'll find them here. By clicking on the three horizontal dots, you can add more app tabs to your interface by choosing from a list of available programs. My video showcases a few of the programs I've been experimenting with recently, including: Planner is a project management tool from Microsoft. Using this tool, you can manage projects and assignments by assigning, tracking, receiving, and responding to them. If you've used other applications to keep track of activities, you're probably used to marking them or making simple lists. Planner, on the other hand, allows for much more sophisticated task monitoring and management (for example, embedding a checklist within an individual task and having that checklist progress show on the task card on your dashboard).

- Shifts are a program created with the needs of front-line employees in mind. As an hourly employee, you can use this to schedule them and they may use Shifts to make requests and such.

- Microsoft also sees Teams as a platform that may be used in a manufacturing environment, in addition to its overall goal of unifying collaboration and communication. Your users may not have email or other applications that they need, but you must still be able interact and cooperate with them.

- For instance, a shop floor worker might need access to particular data that they don't have on hand because they lack internet access or access to such files via their shop floor computer. Instead of trudging across the factory floor, into the office, and praying that the individual they need is at their desk, they can ask a fast inquiry using Teams' chat, voice, or video.

If you go to the Apps page, you'll notice just how many other first- and third-party programs Teams can interact with in addition to those from Microsoft (currently over 400). GitHub,

Cisco WebEx, Trello, Jira, and Adobe Creative Cloud are just a few of the many tools you're likely to recognize and even be using right now. Even if your company already uses Freshdesk for customer support, you can easily integrate it with Teams without having to pick between the two, and reap the benefits of unified functionality across both platforms. For example. If you utilize the correct plugins, your teams may serve as a kind of Swiss Army Knife for your entire application ecosystem, not just for internal communication and collaboration (and, with the right plugins, for communication and collaboration with external users and customers).

Microsoft Teams a collaboration and communication platform

A quick look at the Teams UI, what you'll see and what your end users will have access to will help you get a better sense of what Microsoft

Teams has to offer. When it comes to improving the productivity of your staff, Kelser has been a trusted Microsoft partner for decades in the New England area. Let us know if there's an area where you think Teams may help your company open up or connect your employees in a new way.

Collaborating with External Users

Microsoft Teams makes it easier than ever to collaborate with vendors, suppliers, partners, and other external users. Users can add external users with phone numbers to Teams. Microsoft Teams Connect enables this. Interoperability between Teams for work and Teams for personal accounts enables internal users to communicate with external users. External user collaboration is also possible in Teams via guest access via a personal or official email address. Teams support the cross-posting of announcements between teams and channels. For instance, your suppliers and vendors would be able to communicate with one another via distinct Teams channels or teams.

Manage external access in Microsoft Teams

People outside of your company can use Teams to find, call, chat, and schedule meetings with you. You can also use external access to communicate with people from other businesses that are still using Skype for Business (online and on-premises) and Skype. It's better to employ guest access rather than granting access to folks from other firms if you want them to see your teams and channels.

- There is a necessity to talk to people outside of your organization. Some of the other members of the team, such as Rob@contoSO and

Ann@northWindTraders.com, are also involved in the project. They are working together on a joint effort

As a business owner, you want your employees to be able to communicate with colleagues from other companies via Teams.

- Any Teams user across the world should be able to find and contact you just by typing in your email address.

External access should be planned

Each type of federation's external access policies set controls at the organization and user level. The policy is disabled for all users, regardless of their user level, when an organization does so. Access to the system from the outside is enabled by default. The Teams admin center controls external access at the corporate level. User-level PowerShell access is available for most settings, except for domain limits.

Domains can either be allowed or blocked.

As long as the domains you add to the blocked list aren't added to the authorized list, they are allowed. This rule does not apply if attendees are allowed to remain anonymous during the meeting. External access can be enabled in four ways in the Teams admin area (Users > External access). People from your company will be able to discover each other and communicate, chat, or schedule meetings with people outside of your company in any domain as the default setting for Teams. Both tenants must be able to speak with persons outside of their own tenants in order for your users to use Teams or Skype for Business on any external domains.

It is possible to only allow external access to the domains that you wish by creating an Allow list. After you accomplish this, a list of permitted domains will be created. When this happens, all other domains will be blacklisted as well. For instance: It is possible to add a domain to a list of blocks. All external domains except those you've blacklisted will be accessible. Once you've compiled a list of the websites you don't wish to visit, you're free to visit any other sites you like. You can't ban all foreign domains. If this is the case, no one in your organization can find or communicate with anyone else outside of your organization, no matter what the domain. The Microsoft Teams admin center can be used by administrators to make changes.

Allowing specific web domains

1. Click on External access under Users > External access in the Teams admin panel.

2. Allow only a few external domains under Choose which domains your users are able to access.

3. Click the "Allow domain names" checkbox.

4. To allow a certain domain, enter its domain name in the Domain box and then click done.

5. A domain can be added by clicking the Add a Domain button. Then, press "Save."

Settings allow you to restrict particular domains.

When you're in the Teams admin area, navigate to Users > External Access and click the External Access option. When you're done, click the Save and Close button to save your changes and exit out of the page. Simply select Block domains from here on out. To allow a certain domain, enter its domain name in the Domain box and then click done. Add a domain to block if you wish to restrict access to a different domain.

It's time to save your progress.

It's up to the other tenant whether they accept all external domains or only the ones you specified.

Getting Started with Microsoft Teams

With Microsoft Teams, you have the option of using it in three different ways. To connect with others, you can use the Teams mobile app on your smartphone or tablet, the web-based app or the client installed on your laptop or desktop computer. Things will continue to work the same way as long as you're using Teams the same manner. Please log in to the web-based application to begin. Then, on your desktop, set up the client. Team's web-based version can be accessed by following these procedures.

1. Launch your preferred web browser. Type "Microsoft."Com" in the search box.
2. Log in to Office 365 with the credentials you created when you signed up for the free trial.
3. When you get the option to download Teams or use the web app, select Use the Web App. Instead of using the web app, utilize it instead.

The main Teams app opens on your web browser after you sign in, as illustrated.

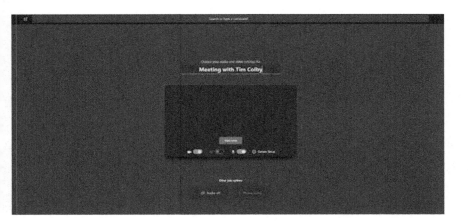

- Using these instructions, you can get the Teams client installed on your computer:

Go to Microsoft.com in your web browser to begin the process. The online app will ask you to log in. If you've previously logged onto your account, you can access an online app called Teams (shown).

- Log in to Teams using the credentials you set up in Chapter 1 if you aren't already logged in to the site

It appears to be this way: 3. Click your profile symbol in the upper-right corner of your screen and select download the Desktop App.

- Save the file on your computer.

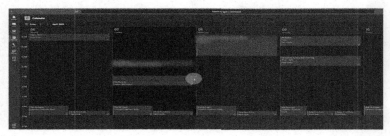

Depending on your needs, you can opt to install desktop or mobile apps from the drop-down box in your profile.

When downloading data, you can instruct your web browser to save it in a specified location on your computer's hard drive. By default, all of your downloaded files will be located in the Downloads folder. You should check your web browser's settings to see where files are saved after downloading an item. Open and run the downloaded Teams installation file. Soon after, you'll be presented with the option to sign in, as indicated by the screenshot.

❖ When you first launch Teams, you'll see a sign-in screen. After you've entered your username, click Sign In.

❖ If you've previously logged in to Teams via a web browser, you won't be prompted for it again.

❖ A message appears informing you that one more step needs to be completed before you can link Teams with Office, as shown in the screenshot.

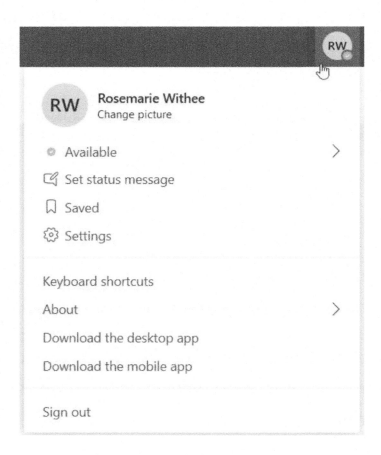

The dialog window informs us that we are now connected to Office. Allow Teams to make modifications to your computer by selecting Let's Do It and then Yes. You can see this in action by starting the Teams application, which connects to Office on your PC in the background. Image

Chapter 3

CREATING YOUR FIRST TEAM AND MANAGING SETTINGS

Collaboration is an essential component of a successful team, which in turn allows you to have a successful workplace. While going over and talking to your coworker is always a fantastic way to do it, there are instances when you need something written down, want to share a file with them, or can't connect with them face to face. This is where the concept of Teams comes into play. We've gone over how to use teams in a variety of ways, including controlling meetings, adding external users as guests, and even creating unique backgrounds. Today, we'll look at how to construct a fresh new Team, and Teams are built using Microsoft Groups.

Note: To create a team, you'll need rights. If you arrive to the phase where you have to create a team and don't see the build a team button, you don't have rights and will need to contact your Administrator for help.

What is a Microsoft 365 Group

A Microsoft 365 Group is a group of people with whom you want to work together and with whom you want to exchange resources effortlessly. Collaboration tools like calendars and document libraries are included in this category. It's a simple matter of adding folks to your Microsoft 365 group to get them access to the team and the resources you've provided. As a result, you'll be able to hold private conversations, file sharing, and note-taking amongst your team members.

Creating Your Team

Putting together a team is a snap. In Microsoft Teams, the first thing you'll want to do is navigate to your Teams tab.

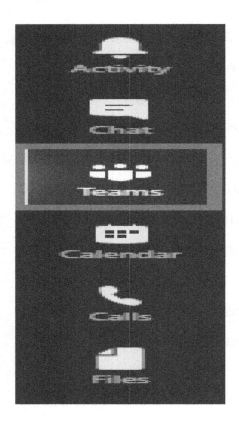

The "Join or form a team" link can be found at the bottom of the page once you've found it.

Once you've done that, go ahead and click "Create Team."

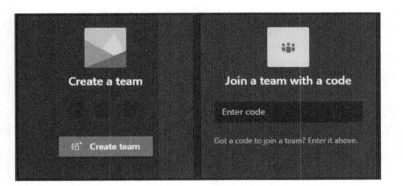

When you click "Create Team," a menu will appear with a number of options. A team can be built from scratch or an existing Microsoft 365 group (SharePoint Online, Outlook, or Yammer) can be used as a source of individuals and permissions for the team. In addition, you'll have access to a wide range of templates for managing projects, hosting events, and onboarding new staff.

Because we're just getting started, we're going to use the "Create from scratch" option for today's lesson.

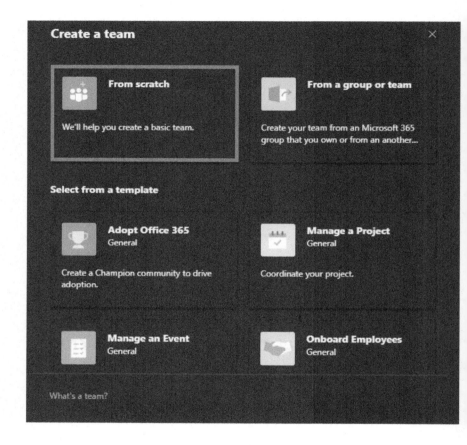

Here are some of the people who can join Teams

When a group is private, only people who were asked to join, or who have the right permissions can join.

- ❖ **It's either public**
- ❖ **org-wide:**
- ❖ **Private**

We are going to pick a Private Team because we only want a few people to work with. You will then be able to name and describe your team! When we name this Blog Team and write about ourselves, we will do that. It's now possible to start making. Your first team has been formed! There are people we want to work with. It's time to add them. You can start filling in who you want to be involved with, and it will start filling in for you. You can then click on the person you want to be involved with. Add groups that have already been made.

Once you've found the people you want to add, you just click "Add" and you can choose which people to add. It's possible to add another owner to the channel if you think that's what the channel needs.

Adding a Channel

Let's get things a little more orderly now that you and your Team have established communication. In a situation when there is just one communication channel, things can grow frantic and make life more difficult for everyone concerned. As a result, we'll be adding a new channel, which will serve as the repository for everything that has been completed and has to be checked out. Adding a channel is as simple as clicking "..." next to the Team and then selecting **"Add a channel."**

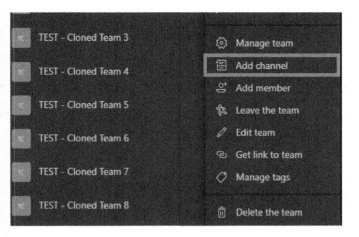

Now all you have to do is give the channel a name, a description, and a privacy level, which can be either "Standard" or "Private":

- In this case, standard means that anybody can see the channel;
- Private means that just a few members of the Team can see it.

Adding people to your Teams

You must be a team manager, team administrator, or organizational administrator (on paid plans) to welcome your teammates into your Koan team. Users on the free tier will be able to create team members and manage their teams). You will be designated as a team administrator automatically if you created the team.

1. To access your team's settings, click the Manage Team icon in the top right corner.
2. Select Members from the team settings.
3. There is a text box under Invite someone to your team where you can input a team member's email address. If the person is already logged in to Koan, their email address will appear in the search bar. If they haven't been invited to Koan yet, you'll need to fill out their entire email address, and we'll send them an email inviting them to join your team and Koan.
4. Click the Invite button! It's that simple.

a. (For Pro and Enterprise plans only) After you've invited someone, you'll have the option of assigning that person to a team role. Member, team manager, team admin, and observer are all possible roles. Go here to discover more about Koan's roles. By selecting the dropdown menu to the right of the user's name, you can modify their role.

That concludes our discussion. We'll give your colleague a Koan invitation to cooperate with you. Have you yet to form your team? To find out how, go here.

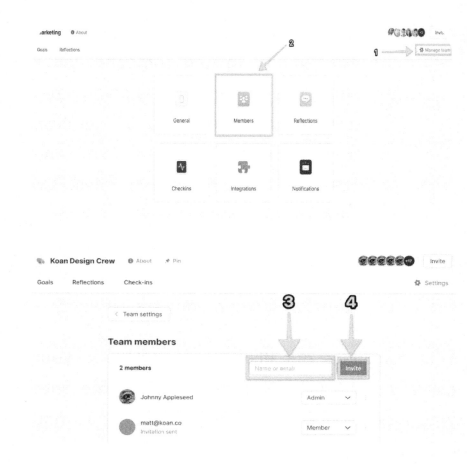

Adding multiple people to Koan on Microsoft Teams

If you're an organizational administrator, you may click Manage Organization > Users > Add Users to add many team members at once or to add users to the tool without issuing invitations.

Add as many users as you like, and choose whether or not to notify them by email when they've been added. It's as simple as adding your user(s).

Welcome Emails vs. Silent Invites:

When you add new users to Koan, you have the option of sending them a welcome email or not.

The email addresses you submitted will receive a Koan invitation regardless of whether or not those people have been joined to teams or if you have finished setting up Koan if you click the Send users a welcome email box. We refer to this as a "Silent Invite" when you don't check Send users a welcome e-mail when adding new users to Koan. If you want to finish setting up the Koan account before allowing users to use it, this is a good option.

If you haven't done, you have two options when it comes to sending out the invitation emails. The three-dot kebab icon appears to the right of the user's name when you return to your list of members via the team settings (Team settings > Members) or organizational settings (Manage Organization > Users). You'll be presented with a drop-down menu from which you can choose whether or not to send the user an invitation.

Microsoft Teams can be used on a variety of platforms, including PCs, Macs, smartphones, and tablets, as well as through a web browser. Installing the client is all that is required for the vast majority of end users to get up and running with Teams. It's as simple as logging in with their login and password when they've installed the Teams client.

A computer's users

The desktop client for Teams is included in Microsoft 365 Apps for business and can be downloaded independently or as part of the subscription.

Support for 32-bit and 64-bit versions of Windows (8.1 or later)

Linux

Windows based server (2012 R2 or later) Operating System for the ARM64-based Mac ARM-based versions of Windows 10 and Chrome OS If you'd want to learn more about using Microsoft Office on a Chromebook, see "How to use Microsoft Office on a Chromebook"

Desktop clients are available for end users to download and install straight from https://teams.microsoft.com/downloads if they have the required local rights. It is not necessary to have administrator privileges on Windows PCs to install the Teams client.

It is up to the IT professional to decide how to distribute the installation files. The Microsoft Endpoint Configuration Manager (Windows) and Jamf Pro are two examples of this type of product (macOS). Team distribution information can be found in the following resources.

The MSI installers for MacOS Jamf Pro Teams on Windows are available in 32-bit, 64-bit, and ARM64 versions. Windows Using the Endpoint Configuration Manager, install Teams. It doesn't matter if you have the 32-bit or the 64-bit version of Windows or Office installed; Teams' x86 architecture will operate. Our recommendation is to use Team's 64-bit version on 64-bit computers. You'll need at least the 4.5 version of the.NET Framework to use Teams. If.NET Framework isn't already installed; the Teams installer will offer to do it for you. Installing the Windows client requires access to the AppData folder in the user's Windows profile. Because it doesn't require elevated rights, installing the client on a user's local profile is much simpler. The following locations in Windows are often visited by this user:

OneDrive for Business

- **Meeting Adding For example,**
- **Percent LocalAppData and**
- **Percent Team Speak.**

In this case, it's: Percentage of AppData OneDrive for Business Percentage

LocalAppData

Users may be asked to enable connectivity with the Windows firewall on their first call through the Teams client. This warning may be ignored by users because the call will still go through even if they dismiss it.

Image Browser client

Full-featured, browser-based client (https://teams.microsoft.com/browser-client) is available. Because webRTC is used by the browser client, no plug-in or download is necessary to use Teams in a browser. A third-party cookie must be enabled in the browser's settings. With the exception of calling and meetings, Teams completely supports the following web browsers. If you're using a desktop computer,

1. Both parties must be using the Teams desktop client in order to share and control shared content during the sharing process. When one or both parties are using Teams in a browser, no control may be exerted. Because of a technological limitation, we're planning to address this issue in the future.

2. When you run Teams in a browser, you can't blur my background. Only the

desktop client of Teams has access to this feature.

3. Only one active speaker can be viewed at a time in browser-based teams meetings.

4. Real-time audio and video traffic cannot be routed through HTTP proxies on Edge RS2 or later.

CHAPTER 4

EXPLORING CHAT, TEAMS AND CHANENNELS, AND APPS

Basics chats in Microsoft's Teams

Everything you do on Teams revolves around chat. Chat has you covered from one-on-one interactions to group chats and channel discussions.

There are a few things to keep in mind:

1. One-on-one or group chats are possible.

You'll want to talk to someone one-on-one from time to time. In some cases, you'll prefer a group conversation. Both options are available in Chat. At the very top of your chat list, you'll see the option to start a new chat. Any type of media can be sent in a chat message, including text messages and emojis as well as animated GIFs and other types of stickers.

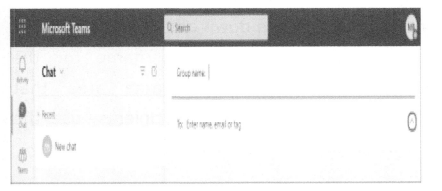

People can talk to each other one-on-one

Once you've chosen new chat and typed in the person's name, write your message in the text box and then choose Send. There's now a chat.

Discussion in a group

When you need to communicate with a small number of people, use a group chat. Begin one the same way you would a one-on-one conversation: At the top of your chat list, click new chat. Select the down arrow to the far right of the to field and type a name for the discussion in the Group name area that appears. To add additional recipients, use the "To" field to enter their names.

The chat can be resumed and more messages can be sent by selecting it from the chat list (whether group or one-on-one).

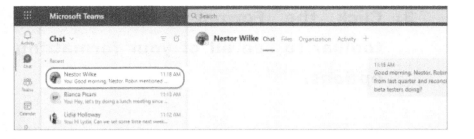

2. Use Shift Enter to start a new line.

Using this method, you can prevent yourself from mistakenly sending a message before you've finished typing it:

Shift Enter can be used to insert a line break at the start of a new paragraph. After you've opened up all of your formatting options, you can just press Enter to start a new paragraph (see step 3 for details).

3. Click the Format button on the toolbar to see all of your formatting options.

You can format messages in many different ways. Format your message by clicking the Format drop-down option that appears beneath the text field where you wish to type it. In this extended view, you can use the formatting options, such as B, I, or U, to make your text bold, italic, or underlined. Highlighting, font size, font color, lists, and more are all included.

Also, under the box, you may add emojis, stickers, schedule a meeting, and more. To find additional apps, select more alternatives and then click on them.

4. People also converse in groups.

"Posts" is the first thing you see when you open a team in Teams. This resembles a massive online chat room. Everyone who has access to the channel can see the messages in Posts.

Depending on your company's culture, you'll have to decide if a message belongs in a channel's Posts page or not. *When using channels, it's crucial to keep in mind that any answers will be linked back to the original message. Reading this will allow anyone to easily follow the conversation's path.* That's why threaded discussions are so wonderful.

Using the little **Reply** button that appears below a message is essential.

Diego Siciliani 3/26/20 9:16 AM
Miriam Graham and team - I've completed my initial review pass on your list of poten
comments in the notes column. I have a couple more names that should probably be

4 replies from you, Miriam, and Grady

↵ Reply

5. It is possible to search for and locate messages in a variety of methods. Different methods of searching for a message may make sense depending on what you recall about its sender or the message's traits.

Use a person's name to look up a live chat

In the app's command box, type the name of the person you'd like to contact. Group chats they're in with you will be listed in your profile. Your one-on-one chat with them or a group conversation can be resumed by selecting their name.

Try to recollect a message that has a keyword in it.

Add a keyword to the app's top command box and press **Enter.** The term will appear in a list of results. Filter the results to see only messages of a specific type. Filter by activity feed by clicking on "Filter by activity feed" Messages, @mentions, answers, and reactions can now be displayed in a variety of ways, making it easier to keep track of them. Right-click on "Feed" and then select "Drop Down Arrow." You can narrow down your search by selecting My Activity.

Find the messages that you've saved.

To save a message, hover over it and **select More options**, then **Store message.**

A list of all your stored messages may be seen by clicking **"Saved"** from the app's upper left-hand corner menu. You can also type /**saved** in the app's command box at the top.

6. Hide or mute conversations.

It is not feasible with Teams to delete an entire chat conversation. You may, however, turn off notifications by hiding or muting the chat. You can learn how to conceal or mute a communication in Teams.

In Teams, starting a chat is a cinch.

A collection of people who work together on Microsoft Teams Choose **Start a new one-on-one** or group chat by clicking on the New Chat button at the top of your chat list.

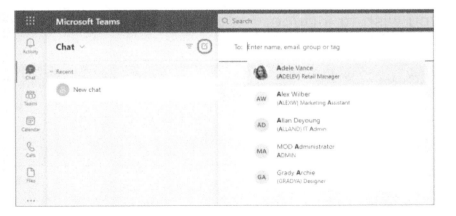

Start a group chat and give it a name.

It's the same process you'd use to open a new chat window.

- To begin a new conversation, there are two options: To create a new chat, click "New" at the top of your chat list.

Take a look at the To drop-down menu by pressing the down arrow on the right of it. Enter a group name in the Group Name area, and then click the Save button.

In the section, enter the names of the persons you wish to include.

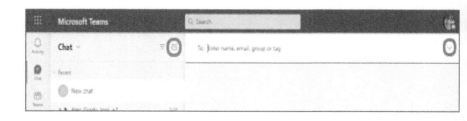

- ✓ Add people to the group chat by entering in their names. '

90

- ✓ It's time to start a fresh conversation. Anyone with access to the group chat can post messages.
- ✓ The maximum number of members in a group chat is 250.

Invite others to join the conversation.

To add more people to a group chat, click the plus (+) button in the upper right corner of Teams. Adding contacts is as simple as typing their names into the text box, selecting how much of their conversation history you wish to include, and clicking on the Add button.

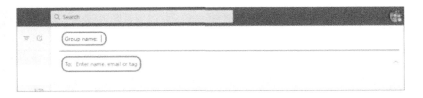

There is a team that saves the entire dialogue, from the first message to the most recent. When a group member leaves, your conversation history is not erased.

How many people are in a group chat

To see a list of everyone in a group chat, select View and then add participants in the discussion headers.

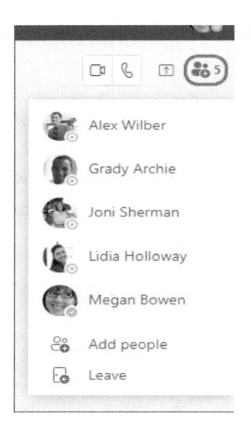

- In TeamSpeak, you can designate a channel to which a message should be delivered.

- When you open a channel in Teams, the Posts tab will be the first one you see there. It's possible to think of posts as part of a larger conversation.

- Access to the Posts page is available to anyone with a subscription to the channel.

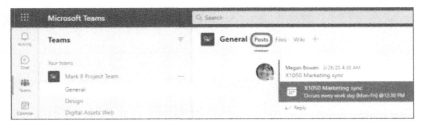

To wrap things up, it's crucial to grasp the link between messages in a channel and the replies that are relevant to the initial message. Reading this will allow anyone to easily follow the conversation's path. That's why threaded discussions are so wonderful. To answer to a message, all you have to do is **click** on the small Reply link that appears underneath it. When you want to start a new conversation in the channel, click the new chat icon in the Posts tab on the lower left.

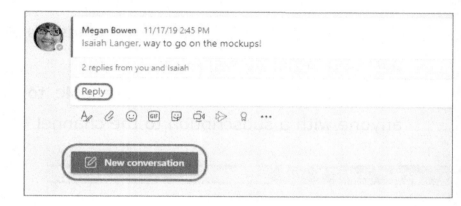

Messages can be typed and formatted in a compose box when responding or starting a new chat. Everyone on a certain communication channel receives a message in one form or another (the entire team).

Click Send after you're finished writing your message. A copy of your message is now available in the channel.

You can pin a chat to the top of the screen or mute, unmute, or conceal a chat in Teams.

When using Teams, you can't completely remove a conversation from your list of conversations, but you can hide or mute it so that you don't receive updates about it. Keep track of the talks that occur frequently so that you don't have to search for them.

Hide a chat in Microsoft Teams

1. Choosing Chat will bring up a list of chats.
2. In the chat you want to hide, **click on More** choices and then > **Hide.**

3. It will take someone else posting a message before a new one appears in the chat. Hidden conversations can be revisited at any time.

Unhide a chat in Microsoft Teams.

1. At the top of Teams, you may find the person you were chatting with by **clicking on the Commands button.** You can type their name into the search

bar and click on their name to find them. That it's buried in the chat history may be seen (which you can choose to show by selecting it).

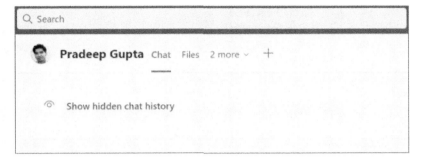

2. To begin with, you'll now see the conversation in your chat list to the left.

3. It's possible to search for it if it doesn't show up right away. When you locate the conversation you wish to reveal, select More options > Unhide from the chat list.

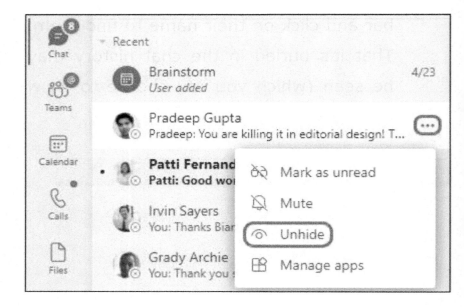

4. **"Show concealed chat history"** can be selected.

Disable a chat in Microsoft Teams.

No one wants to hear from a conversation at certain times of day. If you don't want to hear from a certain chat, you can mute it.

1. **Choosing Chat** will bring up a list of chats.

2. To mute a **chat, click** the more options button next to the conversation you wish to terminate, and then **select Mute.**

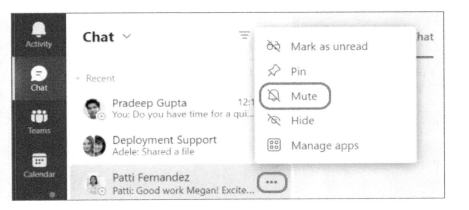

3. You have a final opportunity to change your mind before the deadline. Unmuting it is as simple as selecting it again.

You can detect if a chat has been muted by looking at the icon next to the names of the participants.

1. A message has been pinned to your favorites

2. Put the most current talks at the top of your list so that they are easy to find.

Choosing Chat will bring up a list of chats.

A: As a final step, click on More choices > Pin. You'll never be able to get away from the chat.

Simply pick it again to remove it from the list if you decide otherwise.

Make a team conversation.

It's quick and simple to isolate a one-on-one or group chat into its own window. Afterwards, you can adjust the window's size, move it around, or close it. It's beneficial to accomplish more during a conference call or meeting. As long as you don't want to open up the same conversation repeatedly, you can.

The list of chats

1. When you open a conversation in Teams, you'll see it on your left. To access it, click on the **Chat** tab at the top of the page.
2. Find the conversation you want to participate in.
3. It is possible to select a **pop-out chat** as a third option in step **Double-clicking the chat's** name will bring up a new chat window.

Hovering over a chat

A chat may be hovered over to view what people are saying and what they are doing.

An icon that looks like a window will appear when you hover your mouse pointer over a chat. To launch a new chat window, **click on the button.**

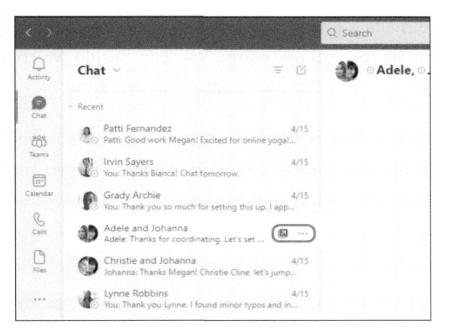

From the context of the dialogue.

In the chat's upper-right corner, **click on Pop-out dialogue.**

Open a new window by **double-clicking** on the picture of the person you want to communicate with on your profile.

You can type whatever you want in the command box to get the job done.

To make a phone call, put /pop in the command line at the top of Teams. You can decide which chat you want to participate in at any time.

Using a chat program, you can make video and audio phone calls. You can make a video or audio call from a chat window.

Pin a chat

1. Click on More options and then Pin to save a conversation. The dialogue can be viewed in the **"Pinned"** section of the list.

You have the option of pinning up to fifteen different conversations.

2. Go to the **chat's** more options and **select Unpin** from the list of drop-down options.

The Teams app allows users to send and receive messages.

Choose "New chat" from the app's main menu. A fresh conversation will begin.

1. Specify the names of the people you wish to communicate with by entering them into To at the top of the new chat.

2. Write your message at the bottom of the chat. Select Format from the drop-down menu.

3. You can send your message to me by clicking Send when you're ready to do so. Everybody who has logged into the chat room can see the messages that have been exchanged.

Get the word out about what you're trying to say.

If you want to carry on a conversation that has already begun (in a group or one-on-one environment), simply select the conversation from the list of already open ones.

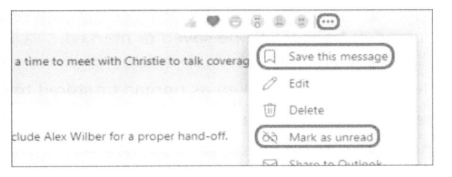

Once a message is out in the world, it can be modified or erased at any time.

Select Edit or Delete from the drop-down box at the upper right of the screen after typing in the relevant message. Enter is the key to save the change.

There is a plethora of ways to respond to a communication once you get it.

Unread messages can be saved or marked.

Messages can be marked as unread or stored to be reviewed at a later time. Additions > This message can be saved or discarded. Mark as unread can be located at the top of the email.

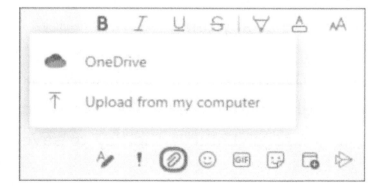

Saved messages can be accessed by clicking on your profile picture at the top of Teams and selecting the Saved option. You can say a lot more when someone reacts to your words. You may quickly respond to any message with an emoji reaction. To pick a message for the entire set, simply hover your cursor over it. Keep an eye on the message's upper-right corner for the notification.

Teams allow you to share a file, a picture, or a link.

Sending files, photos, and links is possible while chatting.

Send a link to a website.

Under the message box, **select Format,** then **insert link.**

- ❖ In order to add a display text or a link to your message, click Insert or Copy and Paste before **clicking Send.**
- ❖ As soon as you send it, you'll get a thumbnail image and a preview of your link in the message.

The ATP Safe Links security ensures that each link you provide or receive is safe for your specific team. As an added precaution, we'll let you know if there's a link you should avoid **clicking on.**

Include a photo or a file.

To insert a file or a photo in a message, select *Choose file* below the message field. Upload a file or a picture from your computer or OneDrive.

By clicking *the Choose file* option, you may select a file from your computer or OneDrive to share in a chat session.

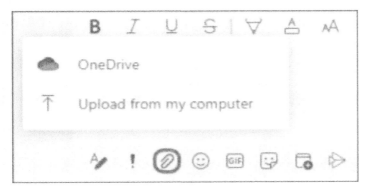

Pick once you've added the display text and the address to the message, **click** Send.

Send a Loop component using the Teams conversation.

When you send a Loop component, everyone in your discussion will be able to edit it in real-time and see the changes immediately. Using a paragraph, table, checklist, or other component as a focus point, your team can work on tasks like co-authoring articles, compiling information, or keeping track of impending steps. Forget about long-winded exchanges.

From the inside of your message, you can collaborate with others.

1. Go to the chat box and start typing a message. In the vicinity of the box, you'll find loop pieces. The box must be empty before doing this. It should be completely free of any text.

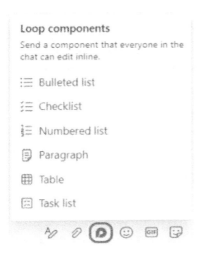

2. Consider the content you want to include in your message before you begin writing.

It's time for the third step. Finally, press the Send button. It will be possible for everyone in the chat room to make changes to the material immediately.

3. Delete and replace the Loop element.
4. Finally, click where you want to add or alter material, and type away!

Add stuff like a @mentions, date or even some code by using the / command when you're editing a post. Use the / sign if you wish to make a comment rather than a change to an existing piece of text. In this way, your comment will be clearly seen.

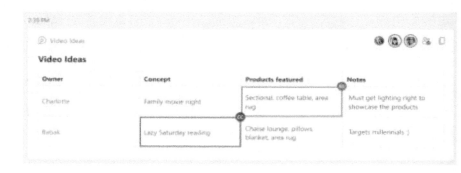

Different colored cursors will appear in your text if someone else is modifying the component at the same time as you are.

An avatar appears in the component's upper right corner to indicate who is currently viewing, editing, or making changes to it. Avatars can be viewed in more detail by hovering your cursor over the image and clicking.

To discover who has access to the component, click "See who has access." There are also people here who have seen the film at least once before.

Share a Loop component in another chat

1. In the upper right corner of the component, click the button that says **"Copy link."**
2. Change chats.
3. Go to where you write a message and press **Ctrl + V** to paste your Loop component into a new chat.

People who were in your first chat and this new one can change the content. The component will always show the most recent changes, no matter where people are working on the project.

View and edit file on Microsoft Team

Whenever you send a chat message with a loop component, the part is saved to OneDrive. How to get from chat to the file on Office.com:

1. At the top of your Loop component, choose the name of the file that you linked.

2. The document will open in Office.com, where you can see and modify it together.

Share your screen in a chat in Teams

You can share your screen with one or more people in Teams when you're conversing. Select Share from the chat controls in the upper-right corner. Select a window to share that program's content, or **choose Desktop** to share everything on your screen. A notification will be sent to the other chat participants, requesting them to accept your screen share. They'll be able to see your screen and continue the conversation once they've done so. Go to your meeting controls and select **Stop sharing** when you're done sharing.

Reply to a specific message in chat

Your chat can be customized so that you can respond to only one specific message at a time. When they read your response, they'll be able to better understand what you're saying. There can be a lot of back-and-forth in discussions. Your one-on-one, group, and meeting discussions become more effective when you respond to a specific message.

The conversation list can be accessed

1. From the left side of Teams by selecting **Chat.**

2. Go to the message you want to respond to in the chat, and then click on the chat you wish to join.

3. **Select More choices** > Reply from the popped-up menu when hovering over the message.

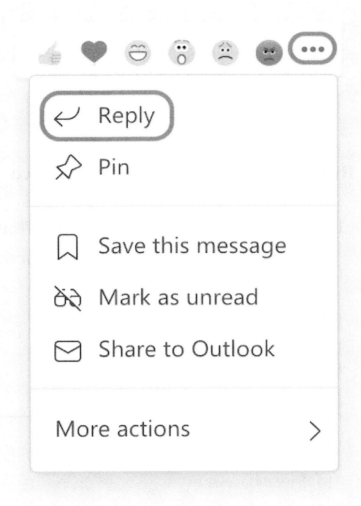

4. Your chosen message will appear in the text field. Select **Send** when you're finished typing your response in the compose box.

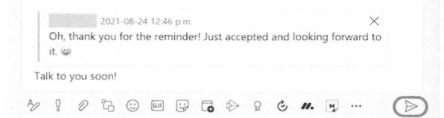

2021-08-24 12:46 p.m.   ✕

Oh, thank you for the reminder! Just accepted and looking forward to it. 😊

Talk to you soon!

Reply to multiple messages at once

1. Select **More options** > **Reply** from a message by hovering your cursor over it.

2. To reply to each message, repeat the first step.

3. As you type, the messages you've selected will appear in the box. Select **Send** when you're finished typing your response in the compose box.

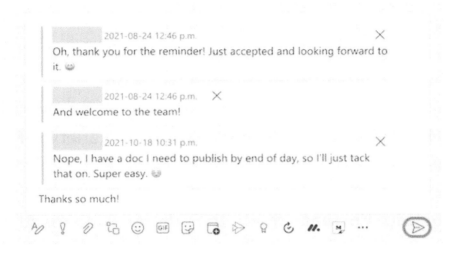

What is the best way to locate the original message?

It's straightforward to discover the original message when you see a reply to a specific message in Chat. Teams will scroll up to the place of that particular message if you select the message preview in the write box or in the conversation.

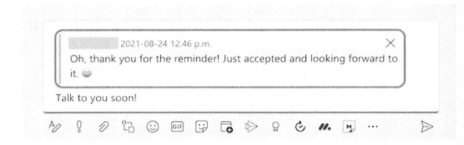

Format a message in Teams

Messages can be formatted in a variety of ways.

Select **Format** from the drop-down menu beneath the compose box to access your formatting options. Select the text you wish to format in this expanded view, then choose an option such as **B, I, or U** to bold, italicize, or underline it.

Highlighting, font size, lists, and other features are also available. **See the more choices section** for extra formatting options, as well as the links below the box for adding a file or inserting fun things like emoji.

Edit or delete a sent message in Teams

Any message you've sent to a chat or channel can be edited.

1. Select **More options** > **Edit** from the message menu.

2. Make any necessary adjustments to your message, and then hit **Enter** to save the modification.

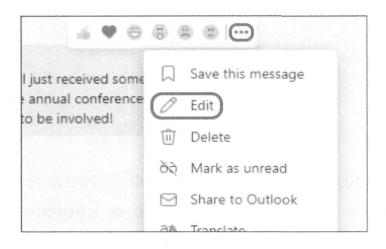

There's no limit to how many times you can edit a message once it's been delivered.

Delete a sent message

Go to the message and **click More options** > Delete if you need to go back and delete something you just sent.

If you haven't yet sent the message, choose **Forma**t to expand the box, and then delete.

Undo a message in Microsoft Teams

Select **Undo** next to the erased message.

Copy and paste in messages

To copy and paste text from a message, use the conventional keyboard operations or right-click.

Commands on the keyboard

- **Ctrl+C** (copy)
- **Ctrl+V** (paste) in Windows (paste)

MaOS

- Command**+C (copy)**
- Command (paste)

It's simple to mark a message as saved or unread if you wish to read it later.

Select More Options > Save this message or **Mark as unread** at the top of the message.

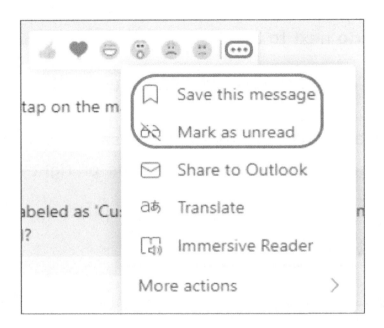

Select your profile image in the upper-right corner of Teams, then Saved to see a list of your **saved** messages.

Mark a message as important or urgent in Teams

Mark your message as important or urgent to ensure that it is received.

Select **Important or Urgent** from the **Set Delivery** Options drop-down menu beneath the compose box.

Your message will now include the words IMPORTANT! or URGENT! You can put files, links, or photographs in the message once it's been sent—whatever you need to get your point clear.

IMPORTANT!

Type a new message

Select **Standard** from your delivery options to undo this option, and the message will be sent as usual. An urgent message alerts a person or group every two minutes for the next 20 minutes, or until they read it. Depending on your organization or group, you'll have to select which messages are urgent.

Pin a chat message to the top of a chat

In a one-on-one or group chat, you might want to pin a certain chat message for future reference. A pinned message is shown at the top of the conversation and remains there until it is withdrawn or changed.

The following are some things to keep in mind with pinned chat messages:

- ➢ When someone pins a message in a conversation, it is visible to everyone in that chat.
- ➢ At any given time, only one message can be pinned.
- ➢ An ongoing chat is unaffected by a pinned message.
- ➢ Anyone in the chat, except guests, has the ability to unpin or change any pinned message.
- ➢ When someone clicks on a pinned message, it will take them to the original message in the chat.

Pin a chat message

1. Hover over the precise message you wish to pin in a chat conversation.
2. Select **more options from** the menu that appears above the notification.

3. **Select Pin** from the More options menu. The pinned message is shown at the top of the conversation. It also includes the author's name and the date or time when it was first published.

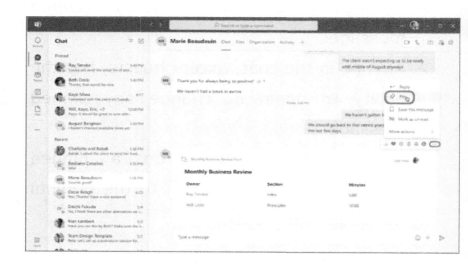

Unpin a pinned chat message

1. Go to the top of the chat and click on the pinned message.

2. Select **More options** > **Unpin** from the drop-down menu.

1. Select **OK** in the confirmation box.

Replace a chat message that has been pinned.

Simply pin a new message to replace an old one that has been pinned. A confirmation message will appear, asking if you wish to replace the original pinned message.

Teams must translate a message.

In Teams, you may adjust the space of your chat messages. You may want to adjust the amount of spacing in chat messages based on the size of your display and your viewing preferences. Teams allow you to change the conversation density to meet your preferences, whether you want to view more text at once or read less text at a more comfortable level.

In compact mode, show more text.

Chat density is set at comfortable mode by default; however you can adjust it in your options if you want to see more text.

1. Select Settings and more **> Settings > General** from the upper-right corner of your screen.
2. **Select Compact** under **Chat density**.

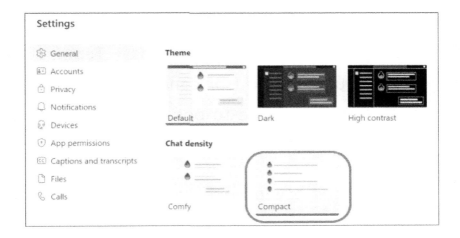

You'll now see more of the chat and a bigger window where you input messages.

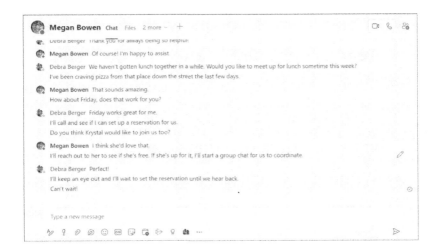

Add or invite people outside your Teams org to a chat

You can add or invite anyone outside of your Teams org who uses Teams, Teams for personal use, Skype (for consumers), or Skype for Business to a one-to-one chat with External Access for Teams.

This includes one-on-one chats as well as new or existing group chats for people that use Teams or Teams for personal use.

The first thing to understand is that

- If you invite someone who doesn't have a Teams account, they'll be sent an invitation to create an unmanaged teams account and then join the chat, complete with all previous conversations.
- Without sending invites, people from various Teams orgs can quickly join each other's chats.
- To engage in a chat, people who use Teams for personal purposes must accept a chat invitation.

- Only a few choices are accessible when a chat is started between a managed Teams org and a Team for personal use account.
- External Access is enabled by default; however it can be disabled or restricted by an organization's administrator, for example, by restricting specific addresses or domains.

If there are any external participants in the discussion, the external label at the top of the chat displays that. In one-to-one and group chat

Anyone who uses Teams, Teams for personal use, Skype, or Skype for Business can be added or invited to a one-to-one conversation from outside your organization.

1. To start a new chat, pick **Chat** on the left side of Teams and then **new chat.**
2. Enter the email address or phone number of the person you wish to chat with.

- Select their name if the name matches, such as someone you've previously invited.
- If there isn't a name match, choose **Externally Search [email address]** to send them a chat invitation. Participant lists, you'll also notice an identifying label next to the names of any external players.

While the status indicator is always available for individuals who use Teams and Skype for Business, it is not accessible to those who solely use Teams for personal purposes or those who only use Skype.

One-on-one conversations can be held with anyone who has access to Teams, Teams for personal use, Skype, or Skype for Business.

Put a message in the bottom text box and click Send to start a conversation.

Join a chat with a teammate from a company that doesn't utilize your company's version of Teams. From outside your organization, you must use Teams or Teams for personal use when inviting people to a group chat. There is the potential for group chat members from multiple organizations that restrict or prevent communication with one another to be included if your organization is allowed to connect with those organizations.

Invite your friends to join a new group chat you've created.

In the same manner as the one-on-one discussion, but with more than one individual, follow the same steps.

Add a group name (optional) before you begin entering a message by clicking the right-hand arrow.

Participate in a group chat already in progress

Only existing chats with at least one external access participant can have additional external access participants. That means creating another group chat with the internal participants and one or more outsiders. Choose or join a group chat to which you wish to invite the participants.

Invite the participants.

From the drop-down menu under your profile photo in the upper right corner of Teams, select View and add participants and then add persons.

Before entering any email addresses or phone numbers in the Add box, decide whether or not you wish to include any chat history.

2. Select the names that appear under Add and then click Add. Those people will be added to the group chat from here on out.

3. You can send a chat invitation to someone if there isn't an instant name match for their email address by selecting Search [email address of person] (no results found). You can start a discussion by typing a message and then clicking Send. In Teams, you can send an emoji, a GIF, or a sticker. The use of emoji, animated GIFs, and stickers can add a personal touch to your correspondence and help you express yourself better. More than 800 new emoji have been added to the gallery, including several that may be modified.

Using emojis in Microsoft Teams

If you want to utilize an emoji in a chat or channel message, here are the steps:

Using the drop-down menu under the message field, select Emoji.

Make a selection from one of the new emoji galleries that are shown at the bottom of the popup window. The first gallery includes hand motions, people, animals, food, travel and places, objects, activities, and symbols.

Select the desired emoji from the emoji collection you've selected.

When you've added the emoji you want, press the Send button.

Embroider your own emojis.

Emojis, including those with grey dots in the corners, can be altered to fit different skin colors. To send a different emoji, simply right-click on an emoji with a grey dot to bring up a menu of choices.

An immediate response can be sent.

You can communicate a lot more with only a few words. The full list of reactions can be found by hovering over a message and selecting the one you want. Find it by looking at its upper right corner.

Send a GIF with motion.

It is as simple as clicking on the drop-down menu next to the text box and selecting GIF as your format. Use the search bar at the top of the window to find specific GIFs (like "cats playing piano"), or browse through the most popular GIFs.

Send a meme or a sticker

Send a meme or sticker to a conversation or channel by selecting Sticker under the box. To see the most popular memes and stickers, select Popular. In Memes, you can look through a variety of sticker options or the entire meme archive. Once you've discovered the perfect one, sirchmply add captions, click Done, and then Send.

Search sticker or a meme.

If you're looking for a sticker or a meme, click Sticker underneath the search box. Once you're in the memes and stickers area, click Popular. Memes and stickers that fit your requirements can then be found by typing in a search term (such as "Grumpy Cat" or "office") at the top of the page.

Make a meme or a sticker that only you could create.

To personalize a meme or sticker, click Sticker in the drop-down menu that appears. Then, select the meme or sticker of your choice. Then click the done button to complete the process. Your updated (hilarious) caption can now be sent to the meme or sticker by selecting Send. You can use the (like) and (love) reactions to convey your feelings or to show that you've taken attention of what someone else has said in your messages. You only have to select the suitable response by hovering your cursor over a chat message. Your selected response will appear just above the message.

People deserve to be commended.

Studies have shown that being recognized for one's accomplishments improves one's mood and increases productivity. Employees and coworkers can be rewarded through the use of praise. Use a channel conversation or a chatroom to spread the word. Take a moment to appreciate the good vibes.

Using the drop-down option that appears beneath where you write a new message or reply, select Praise or Messaging extensions.

Choose a badge.

For each individual you're praising, include their name and a brief description.

When you're done, select "Preview."

Send your message when you're ready.

CHAPTER 5

EXTENDS TEAMS APPS ACROSS MICROSOFT

By changing your code to use the new Microsoft Teams JavaScript client SDK v2 Preview and Microsoft Teams Developer preview manifest, you can test your Teams apps in Microsoft Office and Outlook.

Extend existing Teams personal tabs to Outlook for desktop and web, as well as Office on the web, with this preview (office.com).

Add new Teams search-based messaging extensions to Outlook for desktop and online.

Continue to use the applicable Microsoft Teams developer community channels for feedback and issues. Personal tabs in Office and Outlook for teams You may extend a Teams personal tab application to operate in both Outlook on Windows desktop and the online, as well as

Office on the web, with this preview. In Outlook and Office, your personal tab shows up as an installed program once you side load it to the service.

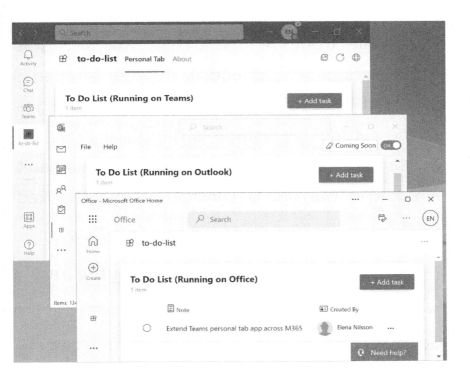

In Outlook, add-ons for Teams messaging.

Using this trial, customers may search and share results in Outlook, as well as Microsoft Teams clients. The Outlook compose message window shows your messaging extension as one of your installed apps after side loading to Teams.

The File tab is where you'll find Backstage.

When you open a Microsoft Office program or select File from the menu bar, the Microsoft Office Backstage view opens. In order to open a file, print it, save it, or make any other changes to the settings backstage is the place to go. In a word, whatever you do to a file that isn't already in the file is considered unauthorized access.

New files can be created by copying and pasting

Select one of the available templates from the drop-down menu, or click on the New button to bring up a list of all available templates.

Open a previously saved file.

The files you've recently worked on are shown on the backstage page. Click the Open button in the left navigation pane to see a list of file locations where you can look for the file you're looking for if it isn't in the Recent Files list. You can "pin" a file to the recent files list so that it is always accessible. File names that have a pin icon next to them appear when you hover over them. Click that to keep the file at the top of the list. Repeatedly clicking on a pinned object will remove it. Remove a file from your recent list by right-clicking it and selecting Remove from list.

Save a Copy.

With Save a Copy, you may quickly create a copy of the current file. In the event that you require a second copy of this file, or if you wish to change a copy of this file without affecting the original, this feature is useful. Find it on the left side of the screen.

Preview instead of printing

Even if you only want to use Print Preview to preview what the file will look like printed, the Print command may be found in the backstage navigation window. For further information, see Printing and print preview.

Collaborating and exchanging ideas

To collaborate on a file, use the Share command. When you're ready to share the file, click Share, then enter the email addresses of the recipients. For more information on file collaboration, see Collaborate on Word documents with real-time co-authoring. Excel and PowerPoint can also be used in the same way.

Office Management

When you open the backstage page, three options can be seen in the lower left corner. It's easy to store and open files from OneDrive and SharePoint with Image Account, a cloud service account management tool. you don't like about your Office software is to provide us feedback. When users use this tool to provide feedback, that information is passed directly through our product teams, who can use it to make future product improvements and enhancements. For further information,

See how can I provide feedback on Microsoft Office?

There are a number of ways in which you can customize your Setting up your app's preferences takes place here. Everything in Office may be customized, including the color scheme, spell check options, editing languages, and the default location of files.

Getting back to work on your manuscript.

You can exit backstage by clicking the Back arrow at the upper left of the navigation pane or by pressing the Escape key on your keyboard.

To a File tab can mean one of the following:

The File tab is a component of the Office Ribbon in Microsoft Word and other Microsoft Office programs that provides access to file functions. Open, Save, Close, Properties, and Recent Files are just a few of the options available from the File tab in Windows 8. Microsoft Word 2010 is depicted in the image to the right. The File tab can be found by clicking on the blue File button in the toolbar's upper-left corner.

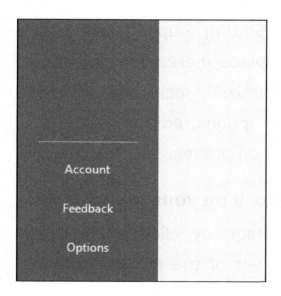

When viewing a computer file's properties, you'll see several tabs at the window's top called "file tabs." New tabs, data, and functionality can be added to the properties window with the use of third-party software. The information listed below is included in each file's tab information.

A list of the file's properties can be found on its File tab.

- The file format (e.g., text file, Word file, HTML file, etc.).
- The file's name.
- The size of the file (in KB, MB or GB).

This information tells you when the file was created and when the last time it were modified.

The file's location.

Is the file protected by any means? (Restrictions on access)

Tabs for files are shown by the red arrows in the illustration below.

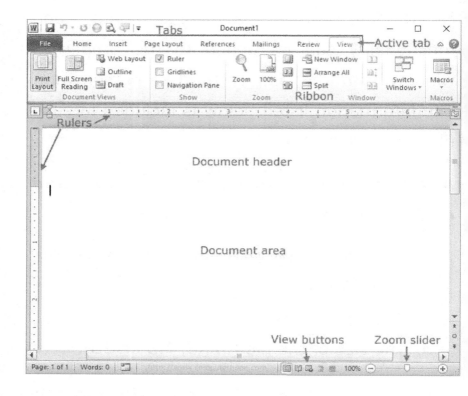

In Teams, create and use a Wiki tab.

Add a Wiki tab to the menu bar.Wiki tabs is available on every channel. Select New Wiki tabs can be created by adding tabs to the existing list of channel tabs. To access Wiki, select it from the list of available tabs. Open a new tab and get to work on your manuscript.

Add content to your Wiki page's content

A Wiki tab has every common formatting choice, such as bold, italic, and underlined text, as well as highlighting, headings, and list items. Each section of a page on your Wiki tab is referred to as a section. Begin by naming your page and then composing the sections. To add a new section, simply mouse over the left side of the page and select Add a new section here.

There is a table of contents on the left-hand side of the page. Quickly go between pages or even organize your files using this method.

Include a section link

Select more options from the drop-down menu. Hover over the section title to see the link.

Send a message from the Wiki tab

In order to have a conversation about a page with a coworker, mention them in a section of the page. Useful when you're waiting for someone else to submit part of your page or for feedback to come in. If you make a mention of someone, a message will display in their Activity Feed. In the message, it's made clear which part of the message they should focus on. Take part in an online conversation with others in a designated area.

The Show section chat button to the right of any section can always be used to initiate an internal debate. It's a good place to ask questions, make comments, or mention your team members. You'll have access to all of the features of your usual compose box, including formatting and attachments. Previously made comments in the tab dialogue will be visible to you. On the top of your screen, you'll see the Show section chat if someone has commented on your wiki page.

Do you know how long it will take to set up?

It only takes a single click to get you up and running. Just open a new tab on your team's preferred channel and add PerfectWiki to it, and you'll be up and running. In terms of exporting data, how straightforward is the process? Archived data is still available to you even if your subscription has expired. There is a good chance you'll see the data as HTML (web page).

A PDF of any page can also be exported at any time, as can a link to the HTML version of any page for anyone outside of Microsoft Teams.

How can I get to a specific page in Microsoft Teams?

Full-text search across all of your team's pages is possible with the "Quick Find" option in Perfect Wiki. This search makes use of both the content and the page titles. The results have been made clear.

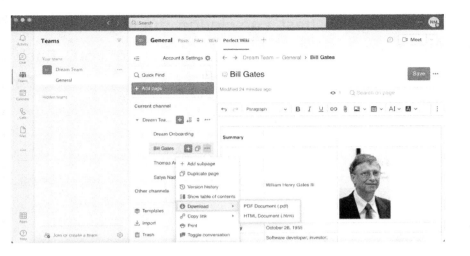

The page search function in Perfect Wiki makes it simple to locate the text you're looking for.

Is there a version for smartphones?

Yes! In fact, you can use the Perfect Wiki mobile app within the Microsoft Teams app to create and update pages directly from your phone. If you're constantly on the go, this is the best solution for you.

For what purpose are you using it?

Choosing the best knowledge management tool for your company is entirely up to you. Each

Popular wiki solution for Microsoft Teams was examined for its advantages and disadvantages. This table summarizes the advantages and disadvantages of each solution so that you can make an informed decision. I hope this essay was useful to you. You may help your coworkers and peers find the best wiki software for their group by distributing this website.

Is there anything else you'd like to know about this app? It's completely free and there are no strings connected, so you may give it a go. It's possible that our policy of unlimited users and complete Microsoft Teams integration will persuade you. You'll find six of the best apps for finding your way around a new city here.

Trip Advisor

When it comes to researching activities, restaurants, hotels, and transportation, TripAdvisor has become one of the most popular websites. In addition to reviews and ratings left by other users, this page also provides details on the area in question. The mobile version of the site is also quite impressive. In an app-like format, all of the website's functions are available. It is possible to pre-download information about a city so that you do not have to use data or search for Wi-Fi when there.

Both iOS and Android versions of the Trip Advisor app are free to download and use.

The Locals are aware of it.

Consider using this app if you wish to get a sense of a city's culture from a local perspective. You won't notice any of the standard tourist traps because the recommendations are all from hand-picked locals. It also has directions and maps to help you go where you want to go. On-the-fly use is also possible. At first, it was just for Amsterdam, but now there are 67 locations in total. Both iOS and Android devices can use the software. City guides cost $3.99 but the app is free to download.

Become closer to each other

If you're planning a trip and want to know what's going on in town, download the Nearify app. It will keep you up to date on forthcoming comedy shows, concerts, parties, and other activities in your neighborhood. It'll even get better at suggesting events you'll enjoy as it gets to know you better. Prepare ahead of time for these situations by receiving notifications from Nearify. Alternatively, you can search for events using the app's many categories. The Nearify app can be downloaded for free from the App Store and Google Play.

Organize a get-together.

If you're a social butterfly, Meetup is a terrific way to meet new people. You can use this app to find folks in your region who share your interests. If you want to learn a language, work out, discuss a topic, or rehearse a dance, you can do it with others. You can also host your own get-together based on the things you're passionate about. If you're in a new city, this could help you meet others and go on adventures together.

Meetings that have already been organized can be found by using Meet up, which is free to download and use. If you wish to create your own groups, you'll need to pay $14.99 per year for an unlimited subscription, or $9.99 per month for the basic organizer. As far as I know, you may use it on any Android or iOS device.

The Culture GPS

In Spanish, the word "you" has both formal and informal meanings. It's not uncommon for Egyptians to ask for your cell phone number from a new acquaintance. Before visiting a new country, it's a good idea to familiarize you with its cultural norms. CultureGPS can help with this. The national culture paradigm of Dutch social psychologist Geert Hofstede will be used to teach you about cultural variations. With the way it's organized, you can easily compare the cultures of various nations.

To use all of the app's functions, you'll need to fork over about $20 for the iOS and Android versions. This is the sixth-place finisher. Google Maps is a one-stop shop for getting around in a new city. There is, of course, a map feature. However, the app can also assist you in locating nearby attractions. You can look for specific types of establishments, such as "restaurants" or "museums." You can also look about your local surroundings. You can also get evaluations from other Google users about the things you've marked on your maps.

CHAPTER 6

EXPLORING TEAMS ON MOBILE DEVICES

The Microsoft Teams Mobile App

You have a few options for installing Teams on your mobile device. The simplest method is to look for the Teams mobile app in the Google Play Store (on Android devices) or the Apple App Store (on iOS devices). Another option is to sign into Teams using your mobile web browser and then press the icon to download the mobile app.

Installing on an iPhone or iPad

To get the Teams mobile app on your iPhone or iPad, follow these steps:

On your **iOS** device, go to the Apple App Store.

In the shop, tap the Search icon and type Microsoft Teams. As indicated, make sure to select the Microsoft app.

To install the app on your smartphone, tap the download link.

Tap the Open button once the software has finished downloading and installing.

Installing on an Android device

To get the Teams mobile app on your Android phone or tablet, follow these steps:

On your Android device, go to the Google Play Store.

In the shop, tap the Search icon and type Microsoft Teams. As indicated, make sure to select the Microsoft app.

To install the app on your smartphone, tap the Install option.

Tap the Open button once the software has finished downloading and installing.

When you first launch the Teams mobile app, you'll see a sign-in screen like the one below, where you can select to sign in to Teams. Enter your Office 365 credentials that you created when you signed up for the Office 365 trial in Chapter 1 by tapping the Sign In button. A team installs the app and gives you some suggestions on how to use it. After you've finished with the tips, you can move on to the next section, where you'll learn how to work with Teams.

Learn how to use the Teams mobile app.

One of the things I like about Teams is that the principles and placement are the same regardless of the client I'm using - the desktop and laptop version or the mobile app. On my Mac, iPad, Android phone, Windows laptop, and iPhone, I've utilized the Teams client. Because

Teams is a relatively new program, Microsoft took advantage of the chance to develop all of the clients at the same time. Because the interfaces are customized for the device you're using, they're slightly different, but if you're familiar with the principles in Teams, you can use any client and feel at ease with it.

The left navigation pane in the Teams online, desktop and laptop apps has been discussed in earlier chapters. Instead of accessing the Teams icons in the left navigation pane, the Teams mobile app features tabs across the bottom of the screen, as illustrated.

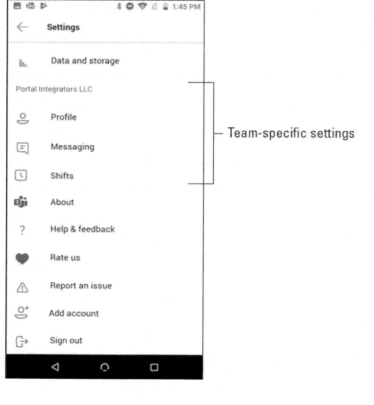

Viewing the Teams mobile app's navigational tabs at the bottom. You access your profile settings by tapping the Settings icon, popularly known as the hamburger menu because of the icon's three layers, which resemble a hamburger. Setting your status and status message, turning on or off notifications, learning about new features, and accessing additional settings related to the mobile app are all available here.

As illustrated in the diagram, three parameters control the settings for the Teams mobile app in general:

- Dark theme: When you enable this feature, the app's colors change to dark. Teams utilizes softer colors by default, but if you're using the app in low-light circumstances, you might prefer the darker hues.

- Notifications: Use this option to change how Teams notifies you. You can setup notifications for incoming calls, missed calls, current calls, chats, likes, and reactions, as well as other notification-related settings. You can also select the hours when Teams should be quiet and not send you alerts.

- Data and storage: It would be great if everyone had infinite data on their mobile devices, but that is regrettably not the case (as I can attest). To help control the data load on your mobile device, you can adjust the quality (size) of photographs you upload, erase temporary files and app data, and clear your conversation history using these options.

Microsoft Teams' general mobile settings.

Additional team-specific parameters are available, as illustrated in the picture that follows this list:

- Profile: This setting allows you to customize your profile photo as well as view your activities, organizational chart, email address, and phone number.

- Messaging: This option allows you to display channels in your chat list. You'll see your channels in addition to your private chats when you tap the Chat tab at the bottom of your mobile screen.

- Shifts: Shifts is a new function that comes from the StaffHub service. Shifts is a feature meant for shift workers. You can set up reminders for your work shifts, schedule when notifications should show before your shifts, and delete data from the shifts app.

- About: This option displays information about the mobile app, including its version, privacy and cookies policies, terms of service, and third-party software notices and information.

- Help & feedback: Select this option to access help information and provide Microsoft feedback on the app.

- Rate us: Use this option to give the app a rating in the appropriate app store.

- Report an issue: Use this option to notify Microsoft about a problem with the app.

- Add account: You can use this setting to add a second account to utilize the program. When I work with clients who have created an account for me under their Office 365 subscription, I do this. My Teams app on my phone allows me to use several accounts.

- Sign out: To sign out of the Teams app, use this setting. This is important if you're giving your phone to someone else and don't want them to use your credentials to access the app.

Tapping your way through Teams

The Teams mobile app is designed to be used by tapping your fingers on the screen of your phone or tablet, just like any other mobile software. A team is intuitive to me, but there are a few changes between using a keyboard and mouse and using your fingers.

Using messages to interact

You can use reactions to add a smiley face, a thumb up, or a variety of other emojis to your chat messages. Furthermore, you can interact with messages in a variety of ways. You are able to;

Save a message to be able to locate and examine it later.

Mark a message as unread so that it appears in Teams as new.

Copy the direct message's link.

Open the message in the immersive reader, which will read it to you and highlight each word as it is spoken.

Turn on the message thread's notifications.

Create a new poll to go along with the message. (This is useful when someone brings up a topic that requires others' input.)

When using Teams on a mobile device, though, hovering your finger isn't an option. Instead, you must tap and hold on the message to access the same option, as demonstrated.

Getting to know how to navigate

As noted earlier in this chapter, navigating the Teams mobile app differs from navigating with a keyboard and mouse. Rather than clicking navigational icons on the left side of the program, these icons are located at the bottom of the app in the mobile edition. Because the amount of space on a mobile device is much smaller than a laptop or desktop computer screen, the experience is designed for mobile devices, which means the flow is slightly different in the mobile app. One important distinction in navigation is that the screens you navigate may take more taps on the screen than mouse clicks. When you tap the Chat button at the bottom of your mobile app, for example, you'll see a list of all the talks you're now engaged in.

The behavior of navigating into your chats on your mobile device is fairly similar to that of the keyboard. If you hit the Teams option, though, you'll see a list of all the teams and channels you have. Then, as indicated in the following diagram, you must press again to open one of those channels. On a wide display, you can see all of the teams and channels at the same time as the channel's associated messages. To enter the channel on the mobile app, you must make a second tap, and to change channels, you must first tap the return symbol and then select a different channel.

Printed in Great Britain
by Amazon

39595926R00108